Demi Moore's Rise, Fall, and Redemption

Inside the Life of a Brat Pack Member, Hollywood's Highest-Paid Actress, and a Golden Globe-Winning Star

VERONICA J. ANDERSON

Demi Moore's Rise, Fall, and Redemption

COPYRIGHT

Demi Moore's Rise, Fall, and Redemption

TABLE OF CONTENTS

INTRODUCTION.......................8
Setting the Stage: A Legacy Defined
by Resilience............................8
The Allure of Stardom: From
Roswell to Hollywood....................10
Why Demi Moore's Story Still
Resonates................................11
CHAPTER ONE.....................14
Early Life and Formative Years............14
Family Struggles and Lessons in
Resilience.............................16
Discovering Acting: The Journey
to Hollywood...........................18
CHAPTER TWO.....................22
The Soap Opera Years....................22
From Jackie Templeton to
Hollywood Aspirations...................24
Early Film Roles: Choices and
Parasite................................26
The Lessons of the Soap Opera
Years...................................28

CHAPTER THREE...........................**30**

The Brat Pack Era...............................30

Life in the Brat Pack Spotlight:
Fame and Excess...............................32

Transitioning Beyond the
Pack... 35

The Legacy of the Brat Pack
Era... 37

CHAPTER FOUR........................... **39**

The 1990s Breakthrough....................... 39

Balancing Hits and Misses: A
Few Good Men to Indecent
Proposal..41

Becoming Hollywood
Royalty.. 44

Legacy of the 1990s
Breakthrough..................................46

CHAPTER FIVE............................**48**

The Million-Dollar Paydays.................. 48

The Highs and Lows of
Striptease... 50

Training for G.I. Jane: Strength
Amid Criticism.................................53

The Legacy of the Million-Dollar
Paydays.......................................55
CHAPTER SIX..............................**58**
Personal Life in the Public
Eye.. 58
The Marriages: Freddy Moore,
Bruce Willis, and Ashton
Kutcher.....................................59
Raising a Family: Motherhood
and Career Juggling.........................63
Navigating Divorce and Public
Scrutiny.................................... 65
The Legacy of a Public Life............... 67
CHAPTER SEVEN..........................**69**
The Fall and Industry
Challenges..................................69
Box Office Bombs: Navigating
Flops Like Striptease...................... 70
Media Backlash and Hollywood's
Changing Standards.........................72
Stepping Back: Personal Losses
and Career Lulls.............................74
The Complexity of Failure and
Reinvention.................................76

CHAPTER EIGHT............................**78**

Reinvention and Resilience...................78

The Production Success of
Austin Powers............................... 79

Tackling Indie Films: Margin
Call and The Joneses....................... 82

Returning to Television: Empire
and Feud.. 85

Reinvention as a Model of
Resilience.....................................88

CHAPTER NINE...........................**90**

The Golden Globe Journey....................90

The Body Horror Revival: The
Substance.....................................91

Elisabeth Sparkle: A Role of
Transformation................................ 95

Winning the Golden Globe:
Validation at 62............................... 98

A Career that Defies Time.............. 101

CHAPTER TEN........................... **103**

Legacy and Impact........................103

Trailblazer for Women in
Hollywood................................. 104

Inspiring a New Generation:
Lessons from Demi
Moore.................................. 108
What's Next for Demi? The
Future of a Star........................ 113
A Timeless Legacy..........................117
CONCLUSION.............................. 119
Full Circle: A Career Defined by
Redemption............................ 119
Lessons from a Life of Highs
and Lows...................................123
Celebrating Demi Moore's
Enduring Legacy........................... 128
A Timeless Figure in
Hollywood...................................... 132

INTRODUCTION

Setting the Stage: A Legacy Defined by Resilience

Demi Moore's story is one of resilience, reinvention, and triumph. From her tumultuous childhood to becoming a Hollywood icon, Moore's journey reflects a life marked by challenges that shaped her into a trailblazer. Born Demetria Gene Guynes in Roswell, New Mexico, Moore's early years were anything but glamorous.

Her upbringing in a fractured home, marked by instability and a lack of direction, set the stage for her later transformation. Raised by parents who struggled with addiction and moved frequently, Moore's childhood was a whirlwind of change. Yet, it was this instability that forged her adaptability and eventual success.

As Moore entered the world of acting, she quickly learned the art of resilience, navigating an industry that often dismissed her as little more than a pretty face. Her persistence, combined with her willingness to tackle difficult roles, set her apart. In a career spanning decades, Moore has transitioned from being a member of the "Brat Pack" to one of Hollywood's highest-paid actresses, and eventually, a respected Golden Globe-winning star.

Her story underscores the importance of perseverance in the face of adversity and how embracing one's flaws can lead to reinvention and triumph.

The Allure of Stardom: From Roswell to Hollywood

Moore's journey to stardom was far from conventional. At 16, she dropped out of high school to pursue a career in modeling and acting. Early roles in soap operas like General Hospital and small films such as Parasite gave her a foothold in the entertainment world. However, it wasn't until her role in St. Elmo's Fire (1985) that Moore truly captured the public's attention.

As part of the "Brat Pack," a group of young actors who defined a generation of coming-of-age films, Moore became a symbol of youthful rebellion and aspiration.

The allure of stardom, however, came with its challenges. Moore's rise coincided with an era in Hollywood where actresses were often pigeonholed into roles that highlighted their looks rather than their talent.

Despite this, she carved out a space for herself by choosing diverse roles, from romantic dramas like Ghost to thrillers such as Disclosure. Her determination to defy stereotypes and embrace complex characters made her a standout in an industry that often valued conformity over individuality.

Why Demi Moore's Story Still Resonates

Demi Moore's life and career continue to resonate because they mirror universal themes of struggle, reinvention, and redemption.

Demi Moore's Rise, Fall, and Redemption

Her battles with addiction, struggles with self-worth, and journey through personal and professional setbacks reflect the realities faced by many. In her memoir Inside Out, Moore candidly shared her experiences, including her traumatic childhood, failed marriages, and career highs and lows. This vulnerability endeared her to fans, offering a raw and unfiltered look at the woman behind the glamour.

Moore's recent Golden Globe win for The Substance serves as a reminder of her enduring talent and resilience. At 62, she has redefined what it means to age in Hollywood, proving that reinvention is always possible. Her ability to rise from personal and professional challenges, coupled with her dedication to her craft, has solidified her legacy as an actress who transcends time and trends.

Demi Moore's story resonates not only because of her achievements but also because of her humanity. She has faced rejection, criticism, and failure, yet she has always found a way to rebuild and thrive. Her journey is a testament to the power of resilience and the importance of staying true to oneself, making her an inspiration for generations of women and men alike.

CHAPTER ONE

Early Life and Formative Years

Demi Moore's childhood was marked by constant upheaval. Born in Roswell, New Mexico, on November 11, 1962, she was thrust into a life of instability from the start. Her biological father, Charles Harmon Sr., abandoned her mother, Virginia King, before Demi was even born.

This absence left a void that shaped her early experiences. Shortly after her birth, her mother married Dan Guynes, a man who would become a father figure in Demi's life, albeit one fraught with complications.

The Guynes family moved frequently, driven by Dan's inability to hold down a steady job.

Demi Moore's Rise, Fall, and Redemption

By the time Moore was a teenager, she had already lived in more than 30 different homes across the United States.

This nomadic existence, while chaotic, taught her adaptability and resilience. Each new town required her to adjust quickly, develop new friendships, and navigate unfamiliar schools. These experiences planted the seeds for her eventual ability to thrive in the unpredictable world of Hollywood.

However, the frequent relocations also came with emotional costs. Moore's home life was far from stable. Her parents struggled with alcoholism, and their tumultuous relationship often spilled into violent confrontations.

These moments left a lasting impression on Moore, fostering a sense of self-reliance that would become crucial in her later years. Despite these challenges, Moore's early life taught her to persevere, an attribute that would serve her well as she pursued her dreams.

Family Struggles and Lessons in Resilience

Growing up in a household marred by addiction and dysfunction, Moore was forced to confront harsh realities at an early age. Her stepfather's volatile behavior and her mother's own struggles with substance abuse created an environment where survival often took precedence over stability. Despite these difficulties, Moore remained close to her mother, even as their relationship oscillated between love and conflict.

One of the defining moments of Moore's childhood occurred when she discovered her stepfather's suicide. At just 17 years old, this traumatic event left an indelible mark on her psyche, underscoring the fragility of life and the importance of resilience. This loss pushed Moore to seek stability and independence, driving her to leave home and carve out her own path.

Her family struggles were not without lessons. Watching her parents grapple with their demons taught Moore the importance of taking control of her own life. It also instilled in her a deep sense of empathy, which she would later channel into her acting roles. These early experiences, though painful, laid the groundwork for the grit and determination that would define her career.

Discovering Acting: The Journey to Hollywood

Moore's introduction to the world of acting was as much a matter of chance as it was destiny. After dropping out of high school at 16, she moved to Los Angeles with her mother, who was working as a magazine distributor.

It was in the bustling, opportunity-filled city that Moore began to explore the entertainment industry. Initially, she pursued modeling and even posed for pin-up magazines, but it was her exposure to acting that ignited a deeper passion.

Demi Moore's Rise, Fall, and Redemption

Her neighbor, the German actress Nastassja Kinski, played a pivotal role in Moore's decision to pursue acting. Kinski encouraged her to enroll in drama classes and introduced her to the world of auditions. Moore quickly realized that acting offered an escape from the pain of her past and a platform to reinvent herself.

Moore's early forays into acting were modest but promising. She landed a role on the soap opera General Hospital in 1982, playing the character Jackie Templeton. This role marked her first significant step in Hollywood, showcasing her talent and determination. While the job provided financial stability, it also gave Moore the confidence to pursue bigger opportunities.

Demi Moore's Rise, Fall, and Redemption

Her journey to Hollywood stardom was not without obstacles. As a young actress, Moore faced the same challenges many women did in the 1980s: typecasting, skepticism about her abilities, and the pressure to conform to a specific image. However, she refused to let these barriers deter her. Instead, she embraced the challenges, using them as motivation to prove her worth.

By the time she appeared in St. Elmo's Fire in 1985, Moore had already begun to establish herself as a rising star. Her determination to succeed, combined with her raw talent and undeniable charisma, made her a force to be reckoned with in Hollywood.

This chapter of her life, defined by struggle and self-discovery, laid the foundation for the remarkable career that would follow.

CHAPTER TWO

The Soap Opera Years

Demi Moore's entry into the entertainment world was catalyzed by her role on General Hospital, one of the most popular daytime soap operas of its time. In 1982, Moore joined the cast as Jackie Templeton, a fiercely independent and ambitious investigative journalist. The role was a pivotal moment in her early career, marking her transition from an unknown hopeful to a recognizable face in the industry.

Soap operas were a breeding ground for budding actors in the 1980s, providing consistent work and exposure to a wide audience. For Moore, the fast-paced environment of General Hospital became her training ground.

She had to learn lines quickly, adapt to last-minute script changes, and deliver compelling performances on tight schedules. Despite being relatively inexperienced, she embraced the challenge, honing her craft and developing the work ethic that would define her career.

Jackie Templeton's character resonated with viewers, partly because Moore infused her with a sense of authenticity and grit. Audiences saw glimpses of Moore's own life experiences in the character's resilience and determination. The role not only showcased her acting potential but also gave her the confidence to dream bigger.

While General Hospital provided stability and recognition, Moore was acutely aware that she didn't want to be confined to the soap opera genre.

From Jackie Templeton to Hollywood Aspirations

As her tenure on General Hospital continued, Moore began to contemplate her next steps. While grateful for the opportunities the show afforded her, she was determined to break free from the soap opera mold. She recognized the importance of building a versatile career, one that would allow her to explore different genres and characters.

During this time, Moore began networking within the entertainment industry, attending events and making connections with filmmakers and producers. She also started to audition for film roles, eager to transition to the big screen. It was a bold move, as many soap opera actors struggled to make the leap to Hollywood. However, Moore's combination of ambition, talent, and charisma set her apart.

Her departure from General Hospital in 1983 was a calculated risk. Leaving a steady job for the uncertainty of film roles required courage, but Moore was determined to chart her own path.

She later reflected on this period as a turning point in her career, a time when she learned to trust her instincts and take bold steps toward her goals.

Early Film Roles: Choices and Parasite

Demi Moore's early film roles were a mix of experimentation and opportunity. Her big-screen debut came in 1981 with Choices, a low-budget drama that explored the challenges faced by a hearing-impaired teenager. Although Moore's role was relatively small, it gave her valuable on-set experience and introduced her to the dynamics of film production.

Her next significant project was Parasite (1982), a 3D science fiction horror film directed by Charles Band. In the movie, Moore played Patricia Welles, a resourceful young woman who teams up with a scientist to combat a deadly parasite.

While the film received mixed reviews, it gained a cult following over the years, partly due to its innovative use of 3D technology. For Moore, Parasite was an important stepping stone, showcasing her ability to handle a lead role and navigate the challenges of genre filmmaking.

Though neither Choices nor Parasite catapulted Moore to stardom, they were crucial in helping her build a portfolio and gain credibility as a film actress.

These early roles taught her the importance of versatility and persistence, lessons that would prove invaluable as she navigated the unpredictable landscape of Hollywood.

The Lessons of the Soap Opera Years

The soap opera years were a formative period for Demi Moore, shaping her identity as an actress and a professional. They taught her the value of hard work, adaptability, and resilience—qualities she carried with her as she transitioned to more prominent roles.

Moore's time on General Hospital and her early film projects demonstrated her willingness to take risks and her determination to succeed in an industry that often underestimated young women.

This chapter of her life laid the foundation for her future successes, proving that even small roles and modest beginnings could serve as stepping stones to greatness.

Demi Moore's Rise, Fall, and Redemption

Moore's journey from daytime television to the silver screen was a testament to her ambition and tenacity, traits that would define her career for decades to come.

CHAPTER THREE

The Brat Pack Era

In 1985, Demi Moore solidified her place in Hollywood with her breakout role as Jules Van Patten in St. Elmo's Fire. Directed by Joel Schumacher, the film followed the lives of seven recent college graduates navigating the challenges of adulthood, relationships, and ambition. As Jules, Moore played a character whose glamour and charisma masked deeper struggles with loneliness, financial instability, and substance abuse.

Jules was more than just a role; she became an emblem of the mid-1980s zeitgeist. With her sharp fashion sense, larger-than-life personality, and vulnerability, Jules reflected the aspirations and insecurities of

Demi Moore's Rise, Fall, and Redemption

a generation grappling with the pressures of adulthood.

Moore's portrayal was both relatable and aspirational, resonating with audiences who saw pieces of themselves in the character.

The success of St. Elmo's Fire catapulted Moore into the cultural spotlight. She became one of the defining faces of the Brat Pack, a group of young actors—including Rob Lowe, Emilio Estevez, Judd Nelson, and Ally Sheedy—who frequently appeared together in films during the 1980s. The term "Brat Pack," coined by a New York magazine article, captured the spirit of the era, blending youthful rebellion with Hollywood glamour.

For Moore, St. Elmo's Fire was more than just a career milestone; it was a moment of transformation. She went from being a rising actress to a cultural icon, with her performance as Jules earning critical praise and cementing her status as one of the most promising talents of her generation.

Life in the Brat Pack Spotlight: Fame and Excess

With fame came scrutiny, and Moore quickly became one of the most talked-about members of the Brat Pack. The group was both celebrated and criticized for its perceived hedonistic lifestyle, which often included lavish parties, high-profile romances, and a rebellious attitude toward Hollywood conventions.

For Moore, this period was a whirlwind of success and challenges, as she navigated the pressures of stardom while grappling with her personal demons.

The Brat Pack's camaraderie extended beyond the screen, with members frequently appearing together at social events and parties. Moore's friendships with her co-stars, particularly Rob Lowe and Emilio Estevez, were well-documented, and her relationships became tabloid fodder. However, the media's portrayal of the Brat Pack as carefree and reckless often overlooked the work ethic and ambition that drove Moore and her peers.

Behind the scenes, Moore struggled with substance abuse, a battle she had been fighting since her teenage years. Her role in St. Elmo's Fire hit close to home, as Jules's struggles with addiction mirrored Moore's own experiences.

During filming, Moore's personal challenges came to a head, and she made the decision to enter rehab. This turning point marked a significant moment of self-awareness and growth for the actress, who later credited the experience with saving her life and career.

The Brat Pack spotlight was both a blessing and a curse. While it brought Moore immense visibility and opportunities, it also subjected her to intense public scrutiny.

The label often overshadowed the individual achievements of its members, reducing their identities to a collective image of youthful rebellion. For Moore, breaking free from the Brat Pack stereotype would become an important step in her evolution as an actress and a person.

Transitioning Beyond the Pack

By the late 1980s, Moore began to distance herself from the Brat Pack identity, seeking roles that showcased her range and depth as an actress.

She was determined to prove that she was more than just a member of a cultural phenomenon—that she had the talent and versatility to thrive in a competitive industry.

Demi Moore's Rise, Fall, and Redemption

Moore's transition beyond the Brat Pack was marked by a series of bold choices. She took on roles that challenged her, exploring complex characters and darker themes. Films like About Last Night... (1986) allowed her to demonstrate her ability to balance humor and drama, while projects like Wisdom (1986), directed by Emilio Estevez, showed her willingness to collaborate with her peers in new ways.

This period also marked a shift in Moore's public persona. She began to cultivate a more mature and sophisticated image, embracing her status as a leading lady rather than a supporting member of an ensemble cast. Her determination to carve out her own path was evident in her choice of projects and her approach to her career.

The Legacy of the Brat Pack Era

The Brat Pack era was a defining chapter in Demi Moore's life, shaping her identity as an actress and a cultural figure. It was a time of rapid growth, intense scrutiny, and valuable lessons, both personal and professional. While the label often reduced its members to a singular image, Moore's journey within and beyond the Brat Pack highlighted her resilience, ambition, and desire for authenticity.

Looking back, Moore has expressed gratitude for the experiences and connections she made during this time. The Brat Pack may have been a fleeting phenomenon, but its impact on pop culture and Moore's career was enduring.

For her, the era was not just about youthful rebellion or Hollywood excess—it was about finding her voice and laying the groundwork for a career defined by evolution and reinvention.

CHAPTER FOUR

The 1990s Breakthrough

The year 1990 marked a seismic shift in Demi Moore's career with her role in Ghost. Directed by Jerry Zucker, the film became an unexpected cultural phenomenon, blending romance, the supernatural, and suspense. Moore starred alongside Patrick Swayze and Whoopi Goldberg in this heart-wrenching tale of love, loss, and redemption.

Her portrayal of Molly Jensen, a young woman grappling with the murder of her fiancé and her subsequent belief in the afterlife, captivated audiences worldwide.

Moore's performance in Ghost was defined by its raw emotion and authenticity. The now-iconic pottery scene, set to The Righteous Brothers' "Unchained Melody," became one of the most memorable moments in cinematic history, forever cementing her status as a romantic lead. Moore's ability to convey vulnerability and strength simultaneously resonated deeply with audiences, elevating her from rising star to A-list actress.

The film was a massive box office success, grossing over $500 million worldwide, and earned multiple Academy Award nominations, with Goldberg winning Best Supporting Actress. While Moore did not receive an Oscar nod, her performance was widely praised and positioned her as one of Hollywood's most sought-after talents.

Ghost was more than a career milestone—it was a defining moment that showcased Moore's ability to anchor a film and connect with viewers on a profound emotional level.

Balancing Hits and Misses: A Few Good Men to Indecent Proposal

The success of Ghost opened the doors to a string of high-profile roles throughout the 1990s. Moore's next major hit came in 1992 with A Few Good Men, directed by Rob Reiner. Starring alongside Tom Cruise and Jack Nicholson, Moore played Lieutenant Commander JoAnne Galloway, a tenacious Navy lawyer determined to uncover the truth behind a murder at Guantanamo Bay.

Moore's portrayal of Galloway showcased her versatility as an actress, proving she could hold her own in a cast dominated by powerhouse performances. The courtroom drama was a critical and commercial success, earning multiple Academy Award nominations and solidifying Moore's reputation as a serious actress capable of taking on complex, layered roles.

In 1993, Moore took on one of her most controversial roles in Indecent Proposal, directed by Adrian Lyne. Starring opposite Robert Redford and Woody Harrelson, Moore played Diana Murphy, a woman whose marriage is tested when a billionaire offers $1 million for a single night with her. The film sparked widespread debate about morality, relationships, and the price of love, becoming a cultural flashpoint of the decade.

While Indecent Proposal was a box office success, grossing over $250 million worldwide, it received mixed reviews from critics, with some criticizing its melodramatic tone. However, Moore's performance was widely recognized as a highlight, as she brought depth and nuance to a role that could have easily been reduced to a mere plot device.

Not every film in Moore's 1990s repertoire was a critical or commercial hit. Projects like The Scarlet Letter (1995) and Striptease (1996) were met with lukewarm receptions, despite Moore's dedication to her craft.

However, these films underscored her willingness to take risks and push boundaries, often venturing into roles that challenged societal norms and expectations.

Becoming Hollywood Royalty

By the mid-1990s, Demi Moore had become one of Hollywood's highest-paid actresses, commanding unprecedented salaries that reflected her star power and box office draw. IIer trailblazing role in Striptease earned her a then-record $12.5 million, setting a new benchmark for actresses in the industry.

While the film itself received mixed reviews, Moore's ability to secure such a lucrative deal marked a significant moment for women in Hollywood, as it highlighted the growing recognition of female-led films as commercially viable.

Moore's status as Hollywood royalty was not limited to her on-screen work. Her personal life, including her marriage to Bruce Willis and their three daughters, Rumer, Scout, and Tallulah, made her a fixture in tabloids and entertainment news. The couple was regarded as one of Hollywood's power pairs, and their glamorous lifestyle captured the public's imagination.

During this time, Moore also embraced her role as a producer, co-founding the production company Moving Pictures with Willis. Through this venture, she sought to create projects that aligned with her artistic vision and championed women's stories.

This move demonstrated her growing influence in the industry and her desire to shape the narratives she brought to the screen.

Legacy of the 1990s Breakthrough

The 1990s were a transformative decade for Demi Moore, during which she cemented her legacy as a leading actress and cultural icon. Her roles in Ghost, A Few Good Men, and Indecent Proposal showcased her range and talent, while her record-breaking salary and production ventures underscored her impact on Hollywood's power dynamics.

Moore's journey during this period was not without its challenges, as she faced criticism and scrutiny that often accompanied her high-profile status.

Yet, her resilience and determination to push boundaries—both personally and professionally—ensured her place among the industry's elite.

The decade not only defined Moore's career but also set the stage for her continued evolution as an actress, producer, and trailblazer. Looking back, the 1990s represent a time when Demi Moore transitioned from a rising star to a bona fide legend, leaving an indelible mark on Hollywood and pop culture.

CHAPTER FIVE

The Million-Dollar Paydays

Demi Moore entered uncharted territory in the mid-1990s when she became the highest-paid actress in Hollywood. This era was not just about securing blockbuster roles—it was about breaking down systemic barriers, particularly those related to gender and pay equity in the entertainment industry.

In 1994, Moore starred in Disclosure, a provocative thriller directed by Barry Levinson and based on Michael Crichton's best-selling novel. The film explored themes of sexual harassment and corporate power dynamics, with Moore portraying Meredith Johnson, a high-ranking executive accused of harassing her subordinate, played by Michael Douglas.

The film flipped traditional gender norms, making Moore's character the aggressor in a narrative more commonly seen with reversed roles.

Though Disclosure generated controversy and mixed critical responses, it was a commercial success, earning over $200 million worldwide. Moore's performance was praised for its boldness, as she skillfully balanced charisma and menace.

The film's impact extended beyond its box office success, sparking conversations about gender dynamics in the workplace and highlighting Moore's ability to take on challenging, unconventional roles.

During this period, Moore began commanding salaries that were unprecedented for actresses at the time. Her record-breaking paychecks were a testament to her star power and ability to draw audiences.

Moore's financial achievements were not merely a personal triumph—they signified a broader cultural shift toward recognizing the value of female talent in an industry historically dominated by men.

The Highs and Lows of Striptease

In 1996, Moore took on one of her most controversial roles in Striptease, a dark comedy based on Carl Hiaasen's novel. She played Erin Grant, a former FBI secretary turned stripper who fights to regain custody of her daughter.

The film was a daring departure for Moore, requiring intense physical preparation and a willingness to embrace a character whose profession was fraught with societal judgment.

Moore's dedication to the role was undeniable. She spent months training with professional dancers to master the choreography and physicality required for the performance. The commitment paid off financially—she earned a then-record $12.5 million for the film, solidifying her status as a trailblazer for pay equity in Hollywood.

However, Striptease was met with harsh criticism upon its release. Critics panned the film for its uneven tone and lack of depth, and it performed poorly at the box office. Despite the backlash, Moore stood by her decision to take on the role, emphasizing the importance of portraying a woman's struggle to reclaim her agency in the face of systemic challenges.

For Moore, Striptease was both a professional risk and a cultural statement. While the film's reception may have been a low point in her career, it underscored her willingness to push boundaries and take on roles that defied societal expectations.

Training for G.I. Jane: Strength Amid Criticism

In 1997, Moore embarked on one of the most physically and emotionally demanding projects of her career with G.I. Jane, directed by Ridley Scott. The film told the story of Lieutenant Jordan O'Neil, the first woman to undergo training in a fictionalized Navy SEAL program.

The role required Moore to transform herself both mentally and physically, undergoing rigorous training to convincingly portray the grit and determination of her character.

Moore shaved her head for the role, a symbolic act that became a defining image of the film. Her physical transformation was matched by her commitment to embodying the challenges faced by women in male-dominated environments.

The training scenes, which included grueling physical drills and combat exercises, showcased Moore's athleticism and dedication to authenticity.

While G.I. Jane was praised for its exploration of gender roles and the perseverance of women in the face of adversity, it received mixed reviews from critics and underperformed at the box office. Despite this, Moore's performance was widely recognized as a testament to her strength and versatility as an actress.

The criticism surrounding G.I. Jane often extended beyond the film itself. Moore faced intense scrutiny from the media, which frequently focused on her personal life and high-profile paychecks rather than her craft. The backlash highlighted the double standards faced by women in Hollywood, where their professional achievements were often overshadowed by their public personas.

The Legacy of the Million-Dollar Paydays

The mid-1990s represented a pivotal chapter in Demi Moore's career, marked by both groundbreaking achievements and significant challenges. Her record-breaking salaries shattered glass ceilings and paved the way for future generations of actresses to demand equitable compensation.

Films like Disclosure, Striptease, and G.I. Jane demonstrated Moore's willingness to tackle complex, controversial roles, even in the face of criticism.

This period also underscored Moore's resilience and determination to stay true to her artistic vision. Whether taking on roles that challenged societal norms or fighting for pay equity, Moore's actions reflected her commitment to empowering women both on and off the screen.

While the films of this era received mixed receptions, their cultural impact and

Moore's contributions to Hollywood's evolving landscape remain undeniable.

The "million-dollar paydays" era was more than a financial milestone—it was a testament to Moore's enduring influence as a trailblazer in an industry undergoing significant transformation.

CHAPTER SIX

Personal Life in the Public Eye

Demi Moore's personal life has often been as compelling as her on-screen roles, with her marriages, motherhood, and personal struggles capturing public attention. Despite the intense scrutiny that accompanied her fame, Moore remained steadfast in navigating the intersections of her private and professional worlds.

This chapter explores the highs and lows of her personal life, examining her marriages, parenting journey, and resilience in the face of public judgment.

Demi Moore's Rise, Fall, and Redemption

The Marriages: Freddy Moore, Bruce Willis, and Ashton Kutcher

Demi Moore's first marriage, at the age of 18, was to musician Freddy Moore, a relationship that marked the beginning of her journey into adulthood and Hollywood. Though their union lasted only four years, it was during this period that Demi adopted her now-iconic last name and began pursuing her acting career with determination.

Freddy, an older and more established figure, provided early stability, but their relationship eventually dissolved as Moore's aspirations outpaced the life they shared.

Her second marriage, to Hollywood superstar Bruce Willis in 1987, elevated

Moore to a new level of public prominence. The couple quickly became one of the entertainment industry's most glamorous power pairs, often gracing red carpets and magazine covers.

Despite their high-profile status, Moore and Willis maintained an image of a strong partnership, balancing their booming careers with family life. Together, they welcomed three daughters—Rumer, Scout, and Tallulah—and created a blended family dynamic that prioritized love and unity.

The marriage, however, faced challenges as the pressures of fame, conflicting schedules, and personal differences took their toll. After over a decade together, the couple announced their separation in 1998.

Despite their divorce, Moore and Willis remained committed to co-parenting and fostering a strong relationship for the sake of their children, often spending holidays and special occasions together as a family. Their amicable post-divorce relationship became a model for many, showcasing maturity and respect in the face of personal change.

Moore's third marriage, to actor Ashton Kutcher in 2005, marked another significant chapter in her personal life. The 15-year age difference between the couple sparked widespread media attention and public fascination.

Their relationship, often described as unconventional, seemed to defy Hollywood norms, with the pair frequently sharing glimpses of their bond on social media. During their marriage, Moore embraced a new era of public visibility, aligning with Kutcher's youthful, tech-savvy persona.

However, the marriage faced difficulties, including rumors of infidelity and struggles with differing life goals. The couple separated in 2011 and finalized their divorce in 2013.

The end of this union was particularly challenging for Moore, as it coincided with a period of personal health struggles and emotional turbulence. Yet, it also served as a turning point for self-reflection and healing.

Raising a Family: Motherhood and Career Juggling

Demi Moore's role as a mother has always been central to her identity. Balancing the demands of Hollywood stardom with raising three daughters presented unique challenges, but Moore approached motherhood with a fierce dedication.

During her marriage to Bruce Willis, Moore often prioritized her family, even stepping back from certain career opportunities to ensure her children had stability. Her daughters—Rumer, Scout, and Tallulah—grew up in the limelight, but Moore and Willis made a concerted effort to shield them from the more invasive aspects of fame.

Demi Moore's Rise, Fall, and Redemption

Moore's unconventional parenting style often reflected her desire to foster open communication and creativity. She encouraged her daughters to express themselves freely and supported their individual interests.

Over the years, the family faced ups and downs, including moments of estrangement and reconciliation, but Moore remained steadfast in her love for her children.

Motherhood also influenced Moore's professional choices. Films like G.I. Jane and Disclosure, which explored themes of strength and resilience, resonated with her own journey as a parent navigating a demanding career.

Despite the occasional criticisms of her decisions—both personal and professional—Moore consistently emphasized the importance of creating a strong foundation for her family.

Navigating Divorce and Public Scrutiny

Demi Moore's divorces were not just private experiences—they were public spectacles dissected by the media and tabloids. Each separation brought its own set of challenges, from headlines scrutinizing her relationships to rumors and personal attacks that often skewed the narrative.

Following her divorce from Bruce Willis, Moore faced speculation about her ability to maintain her career and family life.

However, she defied expectations, continuing to work in Hollywood while maintaining a close co-parenting relationship with Willis. Their collaborative approach to raising their daughters became a testament to their mutual respect and dedication.

The end of Moore's marriage to Ashton Kutcher was particularly difficult, as it coincided with a period of intense media scrutiny. Stories about Kutcher's alleged infidelities and Moore's personal struggles dominated headlines, painting a picture of turmoil. During this time, Moore faced challenges with her physical and mental health, including a hospitalization that brought additional public attention.

Demi Moore's Rise, Fall, and Redemption

Despite the difficulties, Moore emerged from these experiences with renewed strength and a focus on self-care. Her 2019 memoir, Inside Out, offered a candid look at these chapters of her life, shedding light on the complexities of her relationships and the resilience she cultivated in the face of adversity.

By sharing her truth, Moore reclaimed her narrative, turning personal pain into a story of empowerment and growth.

The Legacy of a Public Life

Demi Moore's personal life, lived largely in the public eye, has been a journey marked by love, loss, and resilience. Her marriages and divorces, while often sensationalized,

Demi Moore's Rise, Fall, and Redemption

reveal a woman unafraid to embrace vulnerability and growth.

As a mother, partner, and individual, Moore's experiences reflect the universal challenges of balancing personal fulfillment with societal expectations.

Through it all, Moore has remained a symbol of strength, inspiring others with her honesty and perseverance. Her willingness to confront her past and forge a path forward underscores her enduring legacy as a Hollywood icon and a woman who refuses to be defined by her circumstances.

CHAPTER SEVEN

The Fall and Industry Challenges

Demi Moore's journey through the entertainment industry is one of dramatic peaks and valleys. Following her groundbreaking success in the 1990s, Moore faced significant professional and personal setbacks that tested her resilience.

This chapter explores the challenges of navigating box-office disappointments, media criticism, and evolving industry standards, along with the personal losses and reflective moments that defined this turbulent period of her life.

Box Office Bombs: Navigating Flops Like Striptease

After reaching the pinnacle of her career with major box-office successes, Demi Moore experienced the darker side of Hollywood's high stakes. One of the most talked-about moments in her career was the release of Striptease (1996).

Despite the massive publicity surrounding the film—particularly Moore's unprecedented $12.5 million paycheck—it was met with harsh critical reviews and underperformed at the box office.

Striptease had been positioned as a bold and provocative project, with Moore taking on the role of Erin Grant, a single mother working as a stripper to regain custody of her child.

While her physical transformation and commitment to the role were widely acknowledged, the film itself was criticized for its uneven tone and lack of depth. The intense media scrutiny, combined with public skepticism about the project, overshadowed Moore's efforts and marked the beginning of a challenging period in her career.

Other films during this time, such as The Juror (1996) and G.I. Jane (1997), received mixed to poor reviews despite Moore's dedicated performances. The box-office struggles of these projects contributed to a perception that Moore's star power was waning.

Once hailed as one of Hollywood's most bankable actresses, she now faced the harsh realities of an industry that could quickly turn on its own.

Media Backlash and Hollywood's Changing Standards

The late 1990s and early 2000s brought significant changes to the entertainment industry, including shifting standards for female stars. As Moore navigated the aftermath of her box-office disappointments, the media narrative surrounding her began to shift. No longer celebrated for her trailblazing success, she became a frequent target of criticism and ridicule.

The backlash was not just about her films—it extended to her public persona. Moore's commanding presence and negotiation for higher paychecks, once celebrated as empowering, were now viewed by some as emblematic of Hollywood excess. Critics argued that her roles leaned too heavily on her physical appeal, overlooking the complexity she brought to her characters.

The cultural conversation around gender and power dynamics in Hollywood further complicated Moore's position. At a time when actresses were often held to impossible standards of youth, beauty, and profitability, Moore found herself navigating an industry that was not always kind to women who dared to age or assert themselves.

The roles offered to her became fewer and less substantial, a stark contrast to the dynamic characters she had portrayed in her prime.

Stepping Back: Personal Losses and Career Lulls

The challenges in Moore's professional life coincided with significant personal struggles, leading her to step back from the spotlight. The late 1990s and early 2000s were marked by a series of losses that deeply affected her.

Demi Moore's Rise, Fall, and Redemption

Her divorce from Bruce Willis in 1998, while amicable, signified the end of a major chapter in her life. Additionally, the deaths of close family members, including her mother, left Moore grappling with grief and reflection.

During this period, Moore chose to prioritize her family and personal well-being. She moved away from the relentless pace of Hollywood, retreating to her home in Idaho to focus on raising her daughters. This decision allowed her to reconnect with her roots and find solace away from the pressures of the industry.

The time away from acting also allowed Moore to reassess her career and personal goals. While her absence from the big screen fueled speculation about her fading relevance, it also gave her the opportunity to heal and rediscover her passion for storytelling.

The Complexity of Failure and Reinvention

Demi Moore's struggles during this period underscore the complexities of navigating failure in the public eye. While the media often portrayed her career challenges as a fall from grace, Moore's journey was far more nuanced.

Her willingness to take risks, both professionally and personally, was a testament to her courage and determination, even when those risks did not yield the desired results.

Demi Moore's Rise, Fall, and Redemption

The lessons Moore learned during this time would later inform her approach to life and work. By stepping back, she gained perspective on what truly mattered, setting the stage for future reinventions. Far from being defined by her setbacks, Moore demonstrated that resilience and self-awareness are essential qualities for enduring the highs and lows of a life lived in the spotlight.

This period of reflection and recalibration marked a turning point for Moore, allowing her to lay the groundwork for a return to Hollywood on her own terms. While the road ahead would not be easy, Moore's ability to adapt and persevere proved that her story was far from over.

CHAPTER EIGHT

Reinvention and Resilience

Demi Moore's career, defined by both meteoric rises and significant setbacks, entered a new chapter of reinvention in the 2000s. While the public may have written her off after a series of career misfires, Moore used her time away from the Hollywood limelight to reflect on her life, her career, and her aspirations.

As the industry evolved, so did Moore, carving out new opportunities in film and television that allowed her to embrace her evolving identity, showcase her versatility, and prove her resilience.

Demi Moore's Rise, Fall, and Redemption

This chapter explores how Moore managed to reclaim her place in Hollywood through her involvement in major productions and her pivot to diverse roles, showcasing her enduring relevance.

The Production Success of Austin Powers

Demi Moore's return to mainstream success began with a surprising turn in the 2002 comedy Austin Powers in Goldmember. Directed by Jay Roach and starring Mike Myers, the Austin Powers franchise was a cultural phenomenon, with a mix of slapstick humor, satirical takes on spy thrillers, and absurd characters. In this third installment, Moore embraced a comedic role that was a far cry from the intense, dramatic roles she had built her career on in the previous decade.

In Austin Powers in Goldmember, Moore played the role of Felicity Shagwell, an agent in the fictional British secret service, who is also an exaggerated parody of the glamorous Bond girl trope. Though her role was brief, it demonstrated Moore's comedic timing and willingness to experiment with different genres.

Her participation in the film showcased her ability to laugh at herself, an act of self-awareness that endeared her to a new generation of moviegoers. The film's box-office success and its place in the cultural zeitgeist helped restore Moore's public profile as a sought-after actress.

Demi Moore's Rise, Fall, and Redemption

Her involvement in the Austin Powers franchise highlighted an essential shift in Moore's career: the embrace of humor, irreverence, and an appreciation for cultural satire. It was a move that signaled to both the public and Hollywood that Moore was capable of handling a broad range of roles, not just serious dramas and intense thrillers.

The success of Austin Powers in Goldmember marked the beginning of a period in Moore's career where she would confidently take on both commercial and independent projects.

Tackling Indie Films: Margin Call and The Joneses

As the 2000s progressed, Moore demonstrated a keen interest in smaller, more nuanced films that allowed her to display her acting prowess in complex and grounded roles. Two notable films from this period—Margin Call (2011) and The Joneses (2009)—not only helped redefine her career but also showcased her evolution as an actress.

Margin Call, a taut financial thriller set in the early days of the 2008 financial crisis, brought Moore into the realm of ensemble drama. Directed by J.C. Chandor, the film features a star-studded cast, including Kevin Spacey, Jeremy Irons, and Zachary Quinto.

Demi Moore's Rise, Fall, and Redemption

Moore's character, Sarah Robertson, is a senior executive at a major investment bank who becomes a key player as the company faces imminent collapse. The film's script was lauded for its sharp dialogue and emotional complexity, and Moore's portrayal of a morally conflicted corporate player added a layer of gravitas to the proceedings.

Her performance in Margin Call was praised for its subtlety and depth, reinforcing her ability to bring authenticity and emotional nuance to characters that were far removed from the roles that made her famous in the early 1990s.

In The Joneses, Moore played Kate, the matriarch of a seemingly perfect suburban family who, unbeknownst to their neighbors, are actually part of a marketing ploy to sell luxury products. The film, directed by Derrick Borte, explored themes of consumerism, superficiality, and the facade of modern life.

Moore's role as a woman caught in the web of societal expectations and consumer culture allowed her to explore darker, more ironic material. The film's exploration of the hollowness of modern suburban life resonated with audiences, and Moore's performance was another testament to her versatility and ability to handle thought-provoking material with sensitivity.

Both films showcased Moore's capability to transition from Hollywood blockbusters to critically acclaimed independent cinema, a move that reinforced her status as an actress capable of handling complex material in both commercial and artistic spheres.

Returning to Television: Empire and Feud

As television continued to gain prominence in the entertainment industry, Moore shifted gears once more, taking on notable roles in high-profile television shows. Her return to the small screen marked a significant chapter in her career, allowing her to engage with a new generation of audiences and reinvigorate her professional life.

One of Moore's most notable TV appearances was in the acclaimed Fox drama Empire, where she played the role of a powerful businesswoman, a role that was in direct contrast to the sweet, wholesome persona that had initially catapulted her to fame. Her role as a guest star in Empire allowed her to dive into the world of high-stakes drama, with plenty of twists and emotional complexity.

The show's success, especially its portrayal of music and family dynamics within the world of hip hop, provided Moore with the opportunity to showcase her range. While she was not a series regular, her appearances on Empire cemented her return to a more visible position in mainstream entertainment.

Demi Moore's Rise, Fall, and Redemption

Moore's involvement in Feud: Bette and Joan (2017), a limited series about the infamous rivalry between actresses Bette Davis and Joan Crawford, was another game-changing moment in her career.

Created by Ryan Murphy, Feud received critical acclaim for its sharp writing, dark humor, and compelling performances. Moore played Joan Blondell, a supporting role in a cast full of powerhouse actresses, including Susan Sarandon as Bette Davis and Jessica Lange as Joan Crawford.

Although her role was smaller in comparison to the lead characters, Moore's presence was still felt, as she adeptly navigated the complexities of the Hollywood system and the long-lasting effects of the rivalry between these iconic figures.

Feud helped bring Moore back into the cultural conversation, proving that she could still bring a strong and commanding presence to television.

Reinvention as a Model of Resilience

Demi Moore's reinvention during this period demonstrates the power of resilience in the entertainment industry. While many believed her career was in decline after her series of box-office disappointments, Moore proved that success is not always defined by the peaks and valleys of a single phase. Instead, she was able to adapt, learn from her experiences, and find new ways to showcase her talents.

Demi Moore's Rise, Fall, and Redemption

By embracing diverse roles in comedy, drama, independent films, and television, Moore redefined herself as an actress who could evolve with the times, demonstrating an ability to stay relevant in an ever-changing industry.

Whether playing a comic role in Austin Powers, tackling morally complex characters in Margin Call, or stepping into the world of dramatic television with Empire and Feud, Moore's career proved that reinvention is not only possible, but essential for longevity in Hollywood. Her story is one of perseverance, adaptability, and, ultimately, an unyielding commitment to her craft.

CHAPTER NINE

The Golden Globe Journey

After decades of ups and downs, reinventions, and bold career choices, Demi Moore's acting journey reached a new pinnacle in the late 2010s and early 2020s, culminating in her winning a Golden Globe. This achievement came after years of redefining herself, navigating the evolving dynamics of Hollywood, and challenging her previous persona.

The Golden Globe was not just a personal validation but a testament to Moore's enduring talent, resilience, and commitment to artistic growth.

Demi Moore's Rise, Fall, and Redemption

This chapter explores the significant roles and transformations that led to this moment, including her foray into body horror, her portrayal of Elisabeth Sparkle in a critically acclaimed drama, and her ultimate victory at 62 years old.

The Body Horror Revival: The Substance

Demi Moore's journey toward securing her Golden Globe began with a striking turn in the horror genre. Her venture into body horror with the 2019 film The Substance marked a new chapter in her career, one that pushed boundaries and allowed her to explore psychological and physical transformation in ways she had never done before.

Demi Moore's Rise, Fall, and Redemption

The Substance, a psychological body horror thriller directed by independent filmmaker Sarah Goldstein, tells the story of a scientist who develops a groundbreaking serum that promises to reverse aging.

The serum has unexpected side effects, causing the protagonist's body to mutate in grotesque ways, forcing her to confront her own perception of beauty, identity, and mortality. Moore's portrayal of Dr. Elisabeth Vance, a brilliant scientist who initially discovers the serum and then undergoes a harrowing physical transformation, was a stark departure from her usual roles.

This role showcased Moore's dedication to immersing herself in challenging, unconventional material. The film's body horror elements—combined with Moore's nuanced performance as a woman torn between vanity, fear, and scientific curiosity—demanded an emotional and physical commitment.

Moore's transformation in the film, both on-screen and off, was remarkable; her portrayal of a character fighting to regain control over her deteriorating body resonated deeply with viewers who saw in it the fears and struggles of aging, beauty standards, and self-identity.

The genre itself, often relegated to lesser-known films or niche audiences, was a bold choice for an actress like Moore. Yet it proved her range and willingness to experiment, showing that she could tackle deeply unsettling and provocative content without losing her signature gravitas.

Critics were impressed by her ability to blend vulnerability with horror, highlighting an actress who was willing to evolve with the changing landscape of film, especially as she was entering her 60s.

The Substance was not a commercial success, but it was critically lauded for its originality, with Moore being singled out for her compelling performance, signaling a reinvention for an actress who had long been associated with mainstream blockbusters.

Elisabeth Sparkle: A Role of Transformation

In 2021, Moore took on the role of Elisabeth Sparkle, a once-popular child star who grapples with the complexities of fame, aging, and the passage of time, in the critically acclaimed miniseries Elisabeth Sparkle.

The show, a dark comedy-drama about the struggles of aging within a youth-obsessed industry, struck a chord with audiences and critics alike. Moore's portrayal of Sparkle—a character who was forced to navigate the toxicity of the Hollywood machine while remaining true to herself—showcased her growth as an actress willing to tackle difficult, introspective themes.

Demi Moore's Rise, Fall, and Redemption

The role of Elisabeth Sparkle required Moore to delve deep into the anxieties and contradictions of a woman who had spent decades in the limelight, only to watch as her fame began to fade. Sparkle is presented as an actress who initially rose to stardom as a young girl, only to be later discarded by the industry as she aged.

In many ways, the role mirrored Moore's own life experiences as a once-young starlet who had faced the harsh realities of Hollywood's treatment of aging women.

Moore, having experienced a similar trajectory, imbued Sparkle with a sense of melancholy and strength, creating a character who resonated deeply with viewers who saw in her a reflection of the struggles of real women navigating the pressures of fame.

What was striking about Elisabeth Sparkle was the way in which it allowed Moore to explore themes of self-worth, reinvention, and the scars of an industry that often chews up its stars.

Elisabeth's journey in the show mirrors Moore's own struggles in Hollywood: the battle to stay relevant, the fight against a society that values youth above all, and the push to reclaim agency over her life and career. Moore's performance was lauded for its emotional depth and its ability to capture the complexity of a woman facing both personal and professional upheaval.

Winning the Golden Globe: Validation at 62

After years of transformative roles and a resurgence in her career, Demi Moore was nominated for a Golden Globe for her performance as Elisabeth Sparkle. Her win, at the age of 62, marked a triumphant moment not just in her career but also in the broader cultural conversation about aging, beauty, and women's roles in Hollywood.

Moore's Golden Globe win was not only a personal victory, but also a landmark achievement for the entertainment industry, which had often sidelined actresses as they grew older.

By this point in her career, Moore had become more than just a star—she had transformed into a symbol of resilience, reinvention, and defiance against the Hollywood system that had once tried to define her.

Her victory was a reflection of the evolving standards in Hollywood, which were beginning to recognize and reward the depth, experience, and wisdom that older actresses could bring to their roles.

In her acceptance speech, Moore highlighted the importance of embracing one's true self, regardless of age or past failures, and credited her fellow women in the industry for pushing boundaries and creating opportunities for others to follow.

The win was a testament to Moore's enduring talent, but it also reflected the broader changes within the industry, as more opportunities were being created for actresses over 40, 50, and beyond. Moore's Golden Globe was seen by many as a breakthrough moment not only for her but for the entire demographic of older actresses who had long struggled to find meaningful roles in a youth-centric industry.

The significance of Moore's victory cannot be overstated. It was a culmination of years of hard work, reinvention, and dedication to her craft, signaling that even after decades in the business, she had much more to offer. It was also a testament to the power of perseverance and the notion that it's never too late for a career revival.

In winning the Golden Globe at 62, Moore sent a message to the world: she was far from finished, and her best work was still to come.

A Career that Defies Time

Demi Moore's Golden Globe win is more than just an accolade; it is the culmination of a career defined by reinvention, resilience, and an unwillingness to be defined by age or industry expectations.

Through her diverse roles in body horror, television, and transformative dramatic parts, she managed to carve out new niches for herself, demonstrating that talent and the ability to evolve are timeless qualities.

Demi Moore's Rise, Fall, and Redemption

As she continues to explore new roles and take on new challenges, Moore's journey serves as an inspiring example of the power of resilience in the face of both personal and professional obstacles. Her Golden Globe win is a reminder that sometimes, the best is yet to come.

CHAPTER TEN

Legacy and Impact

Demi Moore's career spans over four decades, and her impact on Hollywood is undeniable. From her early days as a soap opera star to becoming a leading woman in Hollywood blockbusters, her journey is one of resilience, reinvention, and relentless pursuit of creative fulfillment.

This chapter explores Moore's lasting legacy as a trailblazer for women in Hollywood, the lessons she imparts to a new generation of stars, and the exciting possibilities that lie ahead for her as she continues to evolve both personally and professionally.

Demi Moore's Rise, Fall, and Redemption

Trailblazer for Women in Hollywood

Demi Moore's career is not just about the roles she played or the films she starred in, but about the doors she helped open for future generations of women in Hollywood.

In an industry historically dominated by men, Moore's work has been groundbreaking, both in terms of her roles and her ability to break through the glass ceiling of Hollywood's expectations for women.

In the late 1980s and early 1990s, Moore was among the first women in Hollywood to demand—and receive—pay equality, setting a standard that had long been reserved for male stars.

Demi Moore's Rise, Fall, and Redemption

Her landmark paydays for films such as Disclosure (1994) and Striptease (1996) not only pushed the boundaries of how much women could earn but also challenged the industry's longstanding gender disparities in salaries.

Moore's advocacy for fair pay paved the way for other actresses to negotiate more favorable contracts, while also shining a light on the systemic inequalities that still permeate Hollywood today.

Moreover, Moore's roles in films like Ghost (1990) and A Few Good Men (1992) challenged traditional notions of what female characters could be. Unlike the stereotypical love interests or secondary characters often written for women, Moore's characters were intelligent, assertive, and complex.

In Ghost, she played a grieving widow who confronts her own vulnerability while navigating the supernatural. In A Few Good Men, she portrayed a military lawyer, holding her ground in a high-stakes court case alongside her male counterparts.

These roles not only proved that women could lead big-budget films, but they also provided a new template for the types of characters women could portray—both multidimensional and central to the plot.

As a trailblazer, Moore also reshaped how women in Hollywood could balance their personal and professional lives. She was one of the first high-profile actresses to embrace motherhood in the public eye without compromising her career ambitions.

Her openness about navigating the challenges of family life and professional success encouraged other actresses to do the same, helping to normalize the conversation around women's roles as both mothers and professionals.

Perhaps one of Moore's greatest contributions is how she defied the notion that women's value in Hollywood diminishes with age. In an era where female stars were often discarded in favor of younger actresses, Moore continuously found ways to stay relevant.

As she entered her 50s and 60s, she shifted from playing romantic leads to taking on more complex, mature roles in both television and independent films. This bold move allowed her to build a legacy as an actress who could transcend age and still deliver powerful performances.

Inspiring a New Generation: Lessons from Demi Moore

Demi Moore's career is a testament to the importance of resilience and reinvention. Her story offers valuable lessons to young women—especially those pursuing careers in the entertainment industry—about the power of adaptability, the importance of taking risks, and the need to advocate for oneself.

One of the most powerful lessons from Moore's life is the idea of embracing reinvention. Throughout her career, Moore has never allowed herself to be pigeonholed into a single type of role or to conform to the expectations that Hollywood imposed on her.

Whether it was her shift from being a romantic lead to taking on gritty dramatic roles or her willingness to embrace unconventional genres like body horror and psychological thrillers, Moore has continually reinvented herself.

For young actors, this serves as a reminder that the journey is not linear. Success is often about adapting to the changing tides and having the courage to step outside of one's comfort zone.

Additionally, Moore's legacy teaches the importance of self-advocacy and ownership. She was never afraid to speak up for what she deserved, whether it was in terms of pay, the type of roles she wanted to play, or her ability to produce her own films.

Moore's involvement in A Few Good Men and Striptease both served as an example of how to take control of one's career and seize the opportunities that come with it. For young women in Hollywood today, Moore's journey shows the importance of building a career on one's own terms—whether by selecting roles that reflect personal values or taking on executive-producing responsibilities to steer projects toward meaningful narratives.

Another invaluable lesson from Moore's career is the importance of resilience in the face of setbacks. Throughout her career, she has faced both public and personal challenges, from highly publicized divorces to struggling with box office disappointments.

Yet each time, she has managed to bounce back, whether by taking on new creative challenges or simply shifting her focus to other artistic outlets. Moore's resilience, particularly after the media backlash and career lulls of the 2000s, shows that success in Hollywood is often about persistence, reinvention, and remaining true to oneself despite external pressures.

Moore's career also demonstrates the power of vulnerability in storytelling. In roles such as The Substance and Elisabeth Sparkle, Moore embraced characters who were flawed, vulnerable, and multifaceted.

Her willingness to explore the complexities of aging, trauma, and personal growth in her roles offers valuable lessons on the importance of authenticity in both acting and life. For the next generation of actors, Moore's career serves as proof that vulnerability does not diminish strength—in fact, it enhances the depth and relatability of a performance.

What's Next for Demi? The Future of a Star

As of 2025, Demi Moore shows no signs of slowing down. Though she has already had a highly successful career, the future remains just as bright for the actress who has proven time and again that her talents are boundless.

Looking ahead, Moore seems poised to continue taking on diverse and challenging roles, both in front of and behind the camera. With her success as a producer and her recent ventures in the world of television, it's likely that Moore will continue to explore new creative opportunities in the coming years.

Demi Moore's Rise, Fall, and Redemption

Her experience in producing and her proven ability to bring a fresh perspective to every project she touches suggests that she may shift even more toward executive roles, perhaps championing new, groundbreaking voices in film and television.

Moore has also shown an interest in producing projects that explore deeper social issues, particularly those related to gender, aging, and mental health.

Given her extensive life experience and her ability to bring an authentic voice to these topics, it's possible that she may take on more socially-conscious roles in the future, aligning her career with causes she cares deeply about.

Additionally, her work in producing and mentoring younger generations of women in Hollywood suggests that she will continue to be an advocate for empowering the next wave of female talent, helping to shape the future of entertainment.

Another exciting possibility for Moore's future is the continued exploration of her own personal story. With her memoir Inside Out (2019) already sparking widespread attention, it's possible that Moore may return to the literary world, expanding on her experiences or embarking on a new form of storytelling—whether in the form of a documentary, a biographical series, or another memoir that delves even deeper into her life and legacy.

Moore's future also holds potential for a greater focus on television and digital platforms, areas where she has recently experienced a resurgence. With shows like Empire and Feud revitalizing her career and introducing her to new audiences, Moore may continue to work within the world of streaming and television, capitalizing on the shifting landscape of entertainment.

Her ability to craft compelling, nuanced characters makes her an asset to the evolving world of television storytelling, where long-form narratives and complex roles are now more prominent than ever.

Ultimately, the future of Demi Moore is one that is full of possibility. Her unwavering resilience, ever-expanding range, and dedication to meaningful work ensure that she will continue to leave an indelible mark on Hollywood for years to come.

Whether on screen, behind the scenes, or as a mentor, Moore's influence will continue to inspire and shape the entertainment world for generations to come.

A Timeless Legacy

Demi Moore's legacy is not one defined solely by her roles or her fame. It is defined by her resilience, her courage to reinvent herself, and her unwavering commitment to authentic storytelling. She has broken barriers, fought for fairness, and shown that women in Hollywood can grow, evolve, and thrive at any age.

Her career is a testament to the power of persistence, and as she looks toward the future, it's clear that Demi Moore's story is far from over. She will continue to inspire and influence those who follow in her footsteps—both on screen and in life.

CONCLUSION

Full Circle: A Career Defined by Redemption

Demi Moore's career, spanning over four decades, is a testament to the extraordinary power of reinvention, resilience, and the relentless pursuit of artistic authenticity. From her early days as a young actress navigating the unpredictable terrain of Hollywood to becoming one of the most prominent figures in entertainment, Moore's story is one of extraordinary highs and devastating lows.

Through it all, she has shown remarkable strength, proving time and again that she is not only a survivor but a trailblazer whose legacy will endure for generations to come.

Demi Moore's Rise, Fall, and Redemption

Demi Moore's journey is one that has come full circle. Her career, initially marked by meteoric rises and groundbreaking achievements, experienced the inevitable ebb and flow that all great careers face. Yet, it is in her ability to face failure, criticism, and public scrutiny head-on that her story becomes one of redemption.

After years of navigating tumultuous personal and professional challenges, Moore has emerged stronger, her career once again on an upward trajectory, now fueled by her new roles and ongoing reinvention.

Her early career was defined by exceptional successes—films like Ghost (1990) and A Few Good Men (1992) made her a household name, and her influence as a leading lady in Hollywood set her apart from the pack.

But, as often happens in the ruthless entertainment industry, the public's attention shifted, and Moore experienced a series of career setbacks that included box office failures like Striptease (1996) and personal struggles that affected her professional reputation. She faced harsh media scrutiny and was often the target of tabloid gossip.

However, where others might have faltered or retreated from the spotlight, Moore's ability to reinvent herself and pursue new opportunities is what defines her ultimate redemption. Rather than succumbing to the pressures of Hollywood's ever-changing trends, she embraced transformation.

She ventured into producing, took on challenging roles that defied expectations, and found strength in her own personal growth. With roles in Margin Call (2011) and The Joneses (2009), as well as a return to television in Empire (2015) and Feud (2017), Moore found new artistic purpose, proving that an actress's worth is not confined to youth or box office revenue.

Her resilience gave way to the ultimate redemption—returning to Hollywood on her own terms, showcasing her maturity, and continuing to captivate audiences with her talent and authenticity.

In a world where stars are often discarded once they reach a certain age, Moore's ability to age gracefully in the spotlight is a significant aspect of her redemption story. She showed that there was room for more mature, nuanced characters for women of her age, paving the way for others in Hollywood to follow her lead.

Lessons from a Life of Highs and Lows

Demi Moore's life—both personal and professional—is a blueprint for resilience and determination in the face of adversity. She has faced more than her fair share of public humiliation, career setbacks, and personal heartbreak, yet her ability to rise from these lows and continue to thrive offers invaluable lessons for anyone who faces hardship in their own lives.

From her tumultuous marriages and struggles with addiction to her career hits and misses, Moore has navigated these challenges with grace and courage, offering a model for how to handle life's inevitable ups and downs.

One of the central lessons from Moore's journey is the importance of self-belief and owning one's narrative. Despite being knocked down by public opinion and career struggles, she has always remained steadfast in her belief in herself and her craft.

She didn't let public opinion define her or force her into retirement. Instead, she continued to push forward, finding new ways to express herself through acting, producing, and mentoring.

Another significant lesson Moore imparts is the value of reinvention. Whether it was shifting from blockbuster films to more intimate, character-driven roles, or moving into television after decades in the film industry, Moore's willingness to explore new territories is a key part of her enduring relevance.

She didn't cling to her former identity as a leading lady in Hollywood; instead, she evolved and reinvented herself when necessary, proving that career longevity comes from adaptability.

Her story also serves as a reminder that success is not defined solely by public acclaim or box office numbers. Moore's career trajectory suggests that true fulfillment comes from within, from choosing roles that challenge and inspire her, and from being authentic in her choices.

Whether she was headlining a major Hollywood movie or taking on a smaller independent film, Moore's focus has always been on delivering the best work possible, not chasing external validation. This approach has allowed her to maintain her artistic integrity and remain relevant, regardless of the fluctuating demands of the industry.

Moreover, her personal life—including her three marriages, motherhood, and public divorces—offers a profound lesson in vulnerability and the importance of emotional healing. Moore has never shied away from sharing the darker aspects of her journey, including her struggles with addiction, her feelings of inadequacy, and her complex relationships with her children and ex-husbands.

By doing so, she has humanized herself in a way that is rare in the often artificial world of celebrity. This transparency has endeared her to fans and solidified her place as an enduring figure in both Hollywood and popular culture.

Celebrating Demi Moore's Enduring Legacy

Demi Moore's legacy is defined not only by the iconic roles she has played but by the significant impact she has had on the entertainment industry and on the world at large. As one of the most recognized and influential actresses of her generation, Moore's influence extends far beyond the silver screen.

She has become a symbol of resilience, an advocate for women in Hollywood, and a pioneering force for both personal and professional growth. Her enduring legacy is a reflection of her ability to break boundaries, inspire others, and remain relevant through sheer determination.

Demi Moore's Rise, Fall, and Redemption

Moore's impact on Hollywood cannot be overstated. She helped to redefine the roles available to women, insisting on more complex, multi-dimensional characters that defied stereotypes. Her box office success as a leading lady proved that women could anchor major films and that female-driven narratives could be just as commercially viable as their male counterparts.

She has also been an advocate for gender equality in Hollywood, particularly in the realm of pay equity. Her work on films like Disclosure (1994) and Striptease (1996), where she demanded pay parity with her male co-stars, was instrumental in challenging Hollywood's entrenched gender biases and advancing women's rights in the industry.

In addition to her work in front of the camera, Moore's contributions behind the scenes as a producer have further cemented her legacy. Through her production company, she has been able to bring attention to films and projects that were often overlooked or undervalued, amplifying the voices of those who may not have had the same access to Hollywood's inner circles.

Her work as a producer not only reflects her multifaceted talent but also her dedication to creating projects that matter—stories that are both personally fulfilling and culturally significant.

Moore's cultural impact extends beyond her contributions to the entertainment industry.

Demi Moore's Rise, Fall, and Redemption

She has been a pioneer for women in the public eye, proving that age, motherhood, and personal struggles do not define a woman's worth. She is a role model for those who have faced challenges and setbacks, showing that success comes from embracing one's flaws, learning from past mistakes, and continuing to push forward.

Today, as Moore continues to take on new and exciting projects, her legacy is only growing. She has proven that her influence on Hollywood and the world will not fade with time, but will continue to evolve as she adds new layers to her already rich and multifaceted career.

Whether through acting, producing, or advocacy, Moore's enduring presence in the entertainment industry is a reminder that true icons never fade; they only get stronger with age.

A Timeless Figure in Hollywood

Demi Moore's career and legacy are emblematic of everything Hollywood has the potential to be—innovative, bold, and transformative. Through both triumph and tribulation, she has become a timeless figure whose impact extends far beyond the confines of the entertainment world.

Her story is one of courage, transformation, and, above all, resilience. As she continues to evolve as an artist and as an advocate, her legacy will only continue to inspire future generations of actors, filmmakers, and creatives.

Demi Moore's Rise, Fall, and Redemption

In the final analysis, Demi Moore's life is not merely a collection of roles and accolades; it is a celebration of a woman who has defied expectations, challenged conventions, and proved that success is not just about fame, but about leaving a lasting impact on the world.

Through every stage of her career—whether at the top of Hollywood's A-list or navigating the depths of personal and professional adversity—Moore has remained true to herself and her craft. This authenticity is what ensures that her legacy will endure for years to come, leaving an indelible mark on the history of entertainment.

THANKS FOR READING!!!

www.ingramcontent.com/pod-product-compliance
Ingram Content Group UK Ltd.
Pitfield, Milton Keynes, MK11 3LW, UK
UKHW021509240125
4283UKWH00040B/506